TOUCHING BEDROCK

*for Peter Abbs
in gratitude*

TOUCHING BEDROCK

*poems
&
ponderings*

Paul Matthews

Copyright © 2023 Paul Matthews

The moral right of the author has been asserted.

Apart from any fair dealing for the purposes of research or private study, or criticism or review, as permitted under the Copyright, Designs and Patents Act 1988, this publication may only be reproduced, stored or transmitted, in any form or by any means, with the prior permission in writing of the publishers, or in the case of reprographic reproduction in accordance with the terms of licences issued by the Copyright Licensing Agency. Enquiries concerning reproduction outside those terms should be sent to the publishers.

Matador
Unit E2 Airfield Business Park,
Harrison Road, Market Harborough,
Leicestershire. LE16 7UL
Tel: 0116 2792299
Email: books@troubador.co.uk
Web: www.troubador.co.uk/matador
Twitter: @matadorbooks

ISBN 978 1805141 853

British Library Cataloguing in Publication Data.
A catalogue record for this book is available from the British Library.

Printed and bound by CPI Group (UK) Ltd, Croydon, CR0 4YY
Designed and typeset by yellowfish.design

Matador is an imprint of Troubador Publishing Ltd

CONTENTS

FOREWORD 1

1: CANTICLES 3
His Heart Continually 5
Winter's Traces 6
Vespers 7
Stained Glass 8
World Rose 9
And the Lord said 10
One clear lucky night 11
Dewfall 12
Windfall 13
Love's Fabric 14
Articulations 15
Fool Proof 16
Ingrained 17
How many summers 18

2: SEASONS 19
Fierce Valentine 21
In Lockdown 22
Green Man 23
Give Us this Day 24
The Day that's Given 24
I think the song came first 25
A Long Way Down 26
Fragile 27
Rain sent us indoors 27
The Sight of it 28
A Glimpse 29
Mood Music 30
Waiting Outside 31
Solstice 32
Oh how can I drive 32

3: DEPARTURES — 33
Piazza di Spagna — 35
Change of Address — 36
Merry-Go-Round — 37
Following the Link — 38
This Vintage — 39
Being Other Wise — 40
Where do you live now — 42

4: ORACLES — 43
Say this to the King — 45
Shaking the Bay — 46
Minding the Cave — 47
Who Bears us — 48
Lament for Mariupol — 49
House Hold — 50
The Wall Talks — 51
Pondering Gilgamesh — 52
Axe and Pen — 54
Bedrock — 57
Who etched this destiny — 57
Afterword — 58

About the Author — 60
Acknowledgements — 61
Appendix — 63

Foreword

Once this book had found its title the image for the front cover quickly followed – a hand mark from the ice age caves of some 30,000 years ago. But why would whoever made it stencil their intention on the rock-face instead of printing it? The red stuff they breathed around each finger delineates an empty space... no signature, perhaps, but an inborn question: 'Is it me or the echoing cave that speaks'? The bedrock lends its patterning to the hand that touches it

Mind and matter have gone separate ways since then, yet

> *Here in every moment*
> *the world begins.*
> *Past hopes and failures*
> *fade as the morning light*
> *burnishes my cold hands*
> *that attend so patiently.*
> *One holds the page.*
> *The other waits to catch*
> *whatever this first day*
> *in-tends me to write here.*

Canticles

*There is a spell, for instance
in every sea-shell.*
                            (H.D)

His Heart Continually

A little to my left a boy
stands facing the sea,

motionless, with his kite
laughing and plunging.

It is his heart continually
sending red streamers out

as this grey nothing stuff
rolls in from the horizon.

Winter's Traces

A king's son once rode
through this High Gate,

and as his bridle bells
thrilled to the chase

fallow deer pricked
their ears in the wood,

and though
he is centuries dead,

his rash blood muted,
I wish snow to cover

every scent and trace
that no innocent thing

be troubled in Ashdown
this quiet Christmas Eve.

Vespers

As night fell the hermit
knelt in the grove.

His prayer set
the oak leaves quivering,
it came so close.

Only the nightingale
disturbed devotion,
insinuating a strain
to make him blush.

He cursed it
and the grove was hushed.

Stained Glass

Hail Mary in blue and red.
As the sunlight streams
through your rose window
we gaze, content
for Word and Image
to resolve in virgin colours
their old argument.

But, outside your house,
blue sky grows overcast.
Gargoyles spit judgement
on our heads. New Herods
stain your rose with
so much innocent blood.

World Rose

Any rose since Eden might arouse mistrust,
yet its first bud has only to open in the yard
and every evil seems forgiven suddenly.

No worm-tongue mars this moment.

Our fitful senses yield to the scent and
a kindness once our own instils the blood,
strong to undo what deems a rose unworthy.

And the Lord said

Woman, you define
the light. What yearns
in my mute stars
you make articulate.

He never guessed it...
how in her open face
life burns, astonished
at its own nakedness.

One clear lucky night

we lay on the ground
to watch for meteors.

Saw none at first, then
there, then more, each

headlong star — so quick
they were with thought.

The galaxies poured
into our open mouths

then turning slowly home
we gasped again

to see the steady flame of
glow worms in the grass.

Dewfall

Spread a cloth on the grass,
admit night's influence,

then, when morning comes
gather any grace that's given.

Lacking such subtle tincture
how could our craft thrive?

To labour without prayer
lays waste the furrows.

No barley bows grain-laden
if we neglect this courtesy.

The manner of our looking
leaves an imprint there.

May dewfall salve our eyes
and prime the gleam in things.

Dark is more wise than day.
Keep watch while sleeping.

Windfall

Earth, when apples fall,
rouses to strike a tone
prepared since winter.

Round meets round,
as the dark pips honed
in a five-pointed star
gather next year's fire.

We bear God's gravity.

In their sweet interplay
sharp tip and curve
conceive this grace:

'Let Fire underneath lift
Weight to Water, Water
into Air again, and shake
a windfall around our feet'.

Love's Fabric

May the table be set
first with our family bread

then a grace come about us
that whenever we shake

crumbs out at the door
sparrows might carry

sweetness to the sour,
salt to the savourless.

Our cup — it brims over,
blessing the tasks we share.

Say 'tablecloth be spread'
and all hearts can feast here.

    It is love's fabric —
    many strands of us
    woven together.

Articulations

The egg tells us
we are round.

We fall from it
into age. An old

man rocking his
bones remembers

limbs on the bay.
Small shells say

cherish the frail
curve of things.

·

Light sometimes turns outside in.
It looks at us. It lifts the patina
from things our eyes have lidded.

Sometimes the listening air turns
inside outward uttering the word
inlaid in every mundane creature.

Fool Proof

Who appointed me
to this high office?

I do what's needed,
bend my knee
to read the midnight
signature of snails
across my doorstep.

My employment is
to mind the overlap
where self and leaf
braid into the wind
their ifs and maybes.

School unmused me
with its dictations.
Why are we not told
that every small thing
is inlaid with fable?

Fool that I am,
I give my life to this.

Ingrained

The theme we have been given is
wounds and how to heal them;

but why sit with our eyes shut
when a candle burns at the centre?

Things long to be looked at.

The least knot in a floorboard
deflects us from the Path. Its grain

bleeds where the branch was, then
ripples a beauty around it.

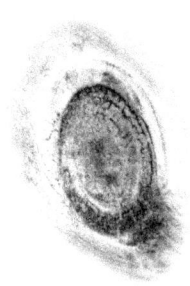

*How many summers
do I have? The wild
rose grazed my skin.*

*I'll tend this plot of earth
with these bare hands.
My blood springs readily.*

Seasons

*Of the seasons,
seamless, a garland.*
             (Ronald Johnson)

Fierce Valentine

Since Candlemas a blue tit has been
flouncing up against our window.

I supposed it was catching insects.
My wife says it's some fierce Valentine
roused by the scarlet of our poinsettia.

Let it be added to the Book of Courtesies.

That's half the story. The missing part
tells how the male bird in love's season
makes a rival of its own reflection.

This blind energy — yes, I remember it.
Let it be written in the Book of Agonies.

In Lockdown

I gaze first thing out over rooftops
and let any lingering dreams
resolve in the mist above the river.

Everything listens. A low ridge
marks the flight path into Gatwick,
but no jet trails veil the horizon.

Friends deliver bread to our door;
primroses everywhere. How then
to delight in it when so many are

gasping for air as the day breaks?
We must stand two metres apart.
If any dream lingers, let love fill
      the distance between.

Green Man

We have hung the green man
on a nail behind the shrubbery,

and though it seems only
a likeness stamped on a tile

the look that he gives says
twine all that you are
into every frond of the garden.

His apple tree is in bloom.
Not a petal has fallen.

But who could befriend him?
He means to lie in the dirt…

the crown of his handiwork
a graveyard where roses run wild.

Give Us this Day

What brings me here
if not this small girl
playing beside a sundial?

She cannot tell the hour
by how a shadow turns.

To pick up stones and
pat them down again is
all the eternity she needs,

and if one happens
to fall beyond her reach
she smiles as I return it
to her outstretched hand.

The Day that's Given

We went out this morning early under blue sky. No clouds were shaping themselves into creatures, and at first not a beast was anywhere in sight but we could hear them, birds ringing in the woods, the chiff-chaff back again. Soon we reached the pond at the bottom of the bluebell dell and watched the surface for signs of animal disturbance. Plenty of dragon-flies there were, but no minnows hungry enough to break the reflection of the birch trees.

So we left that place, and half way up the slope on the other side we paused where two ducks were sleeping, their rounded bills so unlike the jab-a-jabbing beaks of the hens, and then Maria who is training to be a farmer came down the path and we were reluctant to let her pass until she told us a wise thing, so she revealed that the egg-laying chicken has personality while the edible bird has none and that was enough to permit her on her way.

When next we turned we saw two horses standing in a field on the tips of their fingernails. And around yet another bend were the pigs. Pauline said they are psychic and know what awaits them. They seemed more intent though on rootling in the mud for present morsels, or nuzzling milk from their mothers. Sows have more teats than a cow has. None of us could explain it.

On our way back we met Sandra. No need to ask what creature she was because she talked and told us it was her three day task to paint nothing but sheep. Funny, then, that her canvas was totally empty but the sky instead was suddenly full of them and the pond as we passed it this time had a moorhen swimming in the shadows, but we were too intent on coffee to stop and ponder it.

·

*I think the song came first —
cuckoo — and then they wrapped
grey feathers around it.*

A Long Way Down

Hi, sweetheart. Do you remember
the golden toad who visited our patio?

Since then we've discovered the well
our great-grandmothers drank from.
I keep thinking he's down there.

The pebble I dropped
to find out how deep it was
must have ruffled his whiskers.

No, he doesn't need gumboots.

It is very well known though
that toads have a gemstone
tucked between their eyebrows.

What do you think? If we had one
we'd see into tomorrow.

The water is a long way down,
and the pebble hasn't stopped falling.

Fragile

In this photograph most of my relations
are sipping china-tea under the pear tree.

That summer was hot. My grandmother's
dragon teapot guards the endless afternoon.

These delicate cups will never be washed.
These smiles, whatever the tealeaves tell,
        must remain unbroken.

        .

> *Rain sent us indoors.*
> *The garden chairs lean closer*
> *to hear no one talking.*

The Sight of It

This afternoon I drove down
to buy some logs for the winter.
They were all sold out,

but with the rainbow arching
over our lockdown town
it hardly mattered.

When I got home
there was Jenny from next door
waving to her grandchildren.

She hadn't noticed any rainbow,
so I pointed out a strand still
clinging to her chimney pots.

She smiled at the sight of it,
then said 'it isn't polite
for beauty to be pointed at'.

A Glimpse
(for Leah)

Being two years old at the time
you won't recall how the others
went to the opera without us.

Maybe you cried a little.

Left to ourselves I laid out kings
and queens from the card pack.

You stole Jack's knavish heart

and, as I sang to you, a glory
came over your pure face

as if in my poor wrinkled one
you glimpsed some royalty I'd
laid away since childhood.

Mood Music

Wind lifts the oak leaves
    even as they fall.

I can't forget you.

Where the wind comes from,
    where the wind goes.

Someone in the distance sings
    alleluia for the wrong season.

Its griefs and quavers
    filter into the grass.

Don't forget me.

Some people believe it lucky
    to catch a leaf in flight.

Where the wind comes from
    nobody knows.

Waiting Outside

It was not only dry leaves
swirling across the car park.

The November wind kept
tossing a surgical glove

over and over. It was a pale
hand scrabbling in the dust

for something lost, a body
to belong to.

One moment it flipped
sinister as if seeding some

further pestilence;
then, as the wind paused,

I saw how disconsolate
the thing was and wanted

those dark leaves to cradle
that stillborn emptiness.

Solstice

I have stopped the car,
but keep my seatbelt on.

Rain on the roof persists,
that old oblivion.

It lends a momentary gleam
to paint and chrome

then slowly folds us back
into the ground we came from.

.

*Oh, how can I drive
when all this cherry blossom
covers the windscreen.*

Departures

*And to die is different
from what anyone supposed…*
                    (Walt Whitman)

Piazza di Spagna

John Keats died here.
He must have heard
girls giggling oblivious
on the steps outside
as he coughed up blood.

The poet has no address.
They burnt all he had.
A fountain in the square
reiterates the name the
name he wrote in water.

Change of Address
(for Paul Evans)

Thank you for the postcard
you sent me 47 years ago.

Your script slants to the right.
The stamp that you licked

still holds the queen young
in her threepenny corner.

As for the blind-school band
posed on the flip side…

did you choose it at random?
They groove with the blues,

yet nobody thought to say
smile for the camera.

It was you I suppose nudged
this card from its hiding place.

'When will I see you', it says.
It is postmarked midsummer.

Merry-Go-Round

Here's a grey-haired couple
posing astride a painted horse.

The man's togged up in his old
army gear. His wife tucks

daisies into her hatband
for this family photograph.

Round and about they go.
They loved the dance halls,

but the hells of Passchendaele
have crazed their whirligig.

It is a blind horse they ride
backwards though mud and fire,

crying for the daisy chains
that crowned their childhood.

Framed here in black and white
their rag-time days grow quiet.

Following the Link
(for the poet, Jay Ramsay)

Six months before you died you sent me a video about your 'journey with cancer'. There were books behind you, and flowers, and a small glimpse out into further rooms, but your fear of becoming 'a well-known nobody' made me sad.

What strikes me now as I return to it is your firm gaze and how, licking your thumb to turn the pages, you savour the words in silence before you speak them.

I can pause time here. The sharpness of your cheekbones reminds me of I don't quite know... sheer rockface, granite that the grief beneath your smile lays bare — a countenance and encounter I was not prepared for.

I can wind it back, even to when I first met you, angel of fire, stepping from a train near Red Lion Square.

We had our differences — me, hidden in blue; you, strident in your wine–dark shirt, yet caring of the wild flowers underfoot and for fellow travellers.

If we shared things metaphysical I mixed them with foolish word play, but you as a forthright 'legislator of the world' had little time for that.

I am following this link to meet you beyond earthly matters. Your path, being short, was sharp and urgent. Now you smile inside us. The tasting of those pages promises a vintage good for a hundred years.

This Vintage
(for Margli)

We have come to celebrate
our fifty years together,

and, as we lift our glasses,
a sudden flurry in the yard

spins bridal veil and shroud
for every naked statue.

It must be our friend out there
who in these winter nights

died with so much unspent.
What is it about snow?

It makes a home of nowhere,
and he so newly wed is

welcome to slip in unseen
and test this vintage with us.

(Vienna, 3 January 2019)

Being Other Wise
(for Peter Abbs)

You died in a cold season Peter. We were exchanging messages about your new poem, when suddenly you were gone.

What else but to continue, musing if you will on *Les Tres Riches Heures*, scenes of the turning year that I happen to be studying. The Limbourg brothers painted them in honour of the Duc de Berry. Let them interpret you.

'Aproche, aproche' cries his herald, inviting lords and bishops to drink the New Year in. This January scene admits no sign of pestilence, nothing of the lockdown distancing that worried your last days.

And as in thought I savour the duke's red wine, many a rich hour floods back — sweetmeats and poetry shared with you among friends each Tuesday in the Lewes Arms or at our kitchen tables.

February (your birth month) opens upon poor folk huddled against the cold. You wouldn't think it from the picture, but sickness troubled their time, too. The high-minded brothers painted a zodiac to house the faithful and temper whatever Fortune lends.

Your heart warmed to such things. Your head though, hurt by the strictures of some boyhood seminary, set fire to certainties. Passionate scholar that you are, it would not surprise me if you were Abelard.

Or Sappho. Or Socrates. In 'The Story of the Self' that you were writing you take on such guises. It remains unfinished.

The 'metaphysical arts' that you loved were too lofty for some colleagues, but

> 'Already the white chapel on the rock has been expunged:
> high golden cross,
> bronze bell'

…these lines from the bleak poem you sent step down from any *tres riches* ivory towers to a loss of faith and 'blackness petrified'.

I am juggling your autumnal images: The sun 'bleeds down'. 'Tavernas close'. 'Olive tree' and 'shrouded body'. Forget my medieval scenes - this hints at Golgotha, the narrative you could not put down and yet resisted.

Your last message said as much: 'a poem is bigger than our intentions, isn't it'? I drink to that.

As for your final line — 'I am not yet born' — do I read it right… that beyond blind hope our wintry universe shudders and contracts in giving birth?

(see p.65 for the poem referred to)

Where do you live now?
Your earring snagged
my sweater as we parted.

Oracles

*For the Earth which is an intelligence
hath a voice and propensity to speak
in all her parts.*

(Christopher Smart)

Say this to the King:

Men built this oracle
That lies broken here.
Apollo's spring ran dry.

But in the place of ruin
Laurels will rise again.

Tongues, quick now
With a flame within,
Will render dry stone
Into a speaking thing.

Shaking the Bay

Our ancient bay tree quivers
with a hint of storm.

Why then, if trucks upturn
on every highway, do I exult

at this forecast soon to test
the fettle of our window panes?

It must be some longing
for catastrophe, a judgment

on broken promises, and all
the flummery of being human.

Far out there on the Atlantic
the hurricane is roiling in.

This will is more than weather.
We count its isobars, or think

to tame it with a familiar name.
Not so the bay tree. It half recalls

how women shook these boughs,
and prophesied the end of days.

Minding the Cave

She, whoever she was, she
guided us through the painted
caves last summer.

The air made us giddy.
I'm still high on it, imagining
how shadows of earlier visitors

twisted into stags and horses
round the lamp they tended.
She showed us claw marks,

lines in parallel, scored
before ever our kind carried
their frail names in.

We touched bedrock there,
testing where world ends
and the mind begins.

This hallowed place, she said.
Its colours speak in sleep.
Its cries are all about us.

Nobody forgets those horses,
or the bison-woman brooding
in the hollows of the rock-face.

We spun giddy with her
in the flickering light and left
    our footprint.

Who Bears Us

This tin globe we bought is patched
with histories. It fills an empty place.
But who can spin it wise enough
to blend its many warring colours?

I love its coves and tides.

This bauble is named and claimed.
Whoever made it stamped
their trademark where Atlantis was.

It leans precariously.

Some blind nights when the world
rings hollow we incline our heads
to hear the bell towers of Poseidon
rising above the Flood.

'Husband of Earth' he was.
What bond with us does She ask for?

Lament for Mariupol

I can't help questioning the icon
that my mother left me.

She honoured its patriarchs…
their red robes and haloes; but

as the guns shake Mary's Town.
how can I trust these colours?

My own word weighs little.
It is unfit. Yet I must ask

what god is this   wrought here
with the gold of Holy Russia?

He neither frowns nor smiles.
So many have kissed his robe

that the board he's painted on
shows through all semblance.

Let its rough grain bear witness.
Mary's town lies broken.

The crimsons my mother loved
now bloody the green pastures.

House Hold

I the maker of this spell
bring candle book and bell

to exorcise whatever might
trouble this house tonight

One flame to illuminate
corners where shades congregate

Seven tones to rinse the air
of sorrows lingering there

If any fear lurks round about
may the good word cast it out

Here with candle book and bell
this quiet house is held

The Wall Talks

You know who I am.
Every daylight hour
your shadow kicks
at my brickwork.

.

I have held this
ground for you
to test love's word
in the fine anger
that you burn with.

.

If the Earth is round
then with shoes
worn thin you will find
the other side of me.

.

I know who you are.
In a moment neither
dark nor day you might
grave your name here.

Pondering Gilgamesh

The digging up of the 'Gilgamesh' epic two millennia after all trace of it had been lost adds a chapter to its story. It is not mere chance, I mean, that the deciphering of it coincided with the birth of Freud who, delving in his own way, declared that dreams bring hidden motives and desires to light. Gilgamesh, troubled by dreams as he follows the forest paths of his own story, never doubts it; but we (five thousand years after he ruled in Uruk) might do well to open our night eyes a little. It excites me that digging around in deserts we can unearth news still relevant and with such power to move us.

The greatest desire of Gilgamesh is to have his name stamped on brick. It is his destiny, he says; and after his heroic journey through forest and mountains and across the waters of death he feels entitled to *engrave on a stone the whole story*. He commits his name and fame to the earth, confirms it. For good or ill, his word impregnates the clay-mother

The story begins with a great praise for Gilgamesh and for the city wall that he built: *Look at it still today... it has no equal.* It is no random happening that wall-building accompanies the birth of writing. Both acts make a claim to property. If I build walls around me I am saying this plot is mine, and you are outside — you foreigners, you forest folk. Just so if I mark my word into the clay and bake it I might claim the copyright.

Today I walked up a hill and saw notices everywhere — 'private, keep out, beware of the dog, stay on the footpath'. Since Gilgamesh the world has been measured and parcelled out. 'Two thirds God, one third human' he was, and 'one third city, one third garden, and one third field' was the city he ruled over.

However proud he was of his building skills, the divine powers were wary of such activity — so much so that when, in another story, the tower of Babel was under construction they 'confounded' the enterprise. And why? 'Lest they make a name' is their reason for it. The emerging earth-directed consciousness, set on graving its characters into every brick, could no longer participate in the divine mindfulness common before the Flood.

Gilgamesh, intent on fame, forsakes the safety of his brick built measured place and enters the 'Country of the Living' where Humbaba, guardian of the forest, knows from forty leagues distance the wellbeing of each creature. This meeting of self-made man with peripheral dream consciousness leads inevitably to conflict and the felling of trees (such a crisis in our times) is its outer signature.

Gilgamesh and his companion, Enkidu, hesitate over whether to kill Humbaba. Monster he may be, yet to do so risks that the *blaze and glory of light* will be extinguished. This is indeed what happens; the gods give his glamours to the river, to the lion, to the stones, to the mountain and to the queen of hell. What is numinous in nature is lost to us.

The following 'mumblings of Humbaba' feature in an earlier book of mine but find a wider context here:

Axe and Pen

Every time you pick up your pen
it twists into a blade that makes me tremble.

The groves fold beneath it, glades
where I would lie in the sun
as the deer approached unafraid
and licked my cheekbones.

I was the guardian there, each twig
my fingertip. My mind was in it, stretched
ten thousand leagues the seven ways.

I remember the day you swung my gate open
crying *I will stamp my name in this place
lest oblivion take me.*

Ah, but it was my place, my Country
of the Living. I had a woman's eyes,
ten thousand this way that way, and you
shied yours away because I lacked alphabets.

I sent you visions, beautiful and wild;
but when you stepped close to the heart of
my abode you couldn't keep your eyelids open

for you are a man mindful of your name,
and in my place an epithet soon loses itself
among the many syllables the leaves are busy with.

> *Humbaba* is my name, murmur of winds, hubbub
> of baby talk. All the time you are writing
> I am the shadow at your shoulder saying
> *axe and pen, they share a handle.*
>
> I had seven splendours once.
> They are lumbered now in the cold
> catalogue of things; and as you sigh for fame
> you seldom hear the rustlings of my country.

~

It is a tragic tale. These battles between city and forest dweller, between lettered and unlettered, between the rampant masculine principle and the ancient feminine are markers of the descent into 5000 years of the dark Kali Yuga from which only now we are emerging – tragic, but not meaningless. There is indeed a destiny in the loss that Gilgamesh suffers, and the story hints at it.

The act of writing is both result and cause of our self-consciousness. I scrawl words on this paper, read them then think 'oh, I am a somebody'. But, if we start bragging of our exploits, death and all that tests our identity rise up to counter it. So it is with Enkidu. He overhears the Gods declaring that as consequence of Humbaba's death he too must die. *I weep for Enkidu, my friend, bitterly moaning* is how Gilgamesh's lament begins. The story turns on it. In this outpouring of personal love Gilgamesh becomes (as I understand it) more human than the 'one third' that we encounter in earlier pages.

Desperate to cross the waters of death, he persuades the ferryman, 'Servant of Two-Thirds', to carry him over. There he meets Utnapishtim who, retaining an all-embracing consciousness from before the Flood, tells Gilgamesh how the Gods, distracted by the noise that humans make, returned them to the mud they were made from. Read the baked clay tablet in the British Museum for further details… not easy, but the place itself provides an opportunity for standing quietly.

Gilgamesh, known to be the fifth king after that Deluge (and all too human) is unable to stay awake for the seven days and nights required to win the secrets of eternal life. The decaying bread loaves baked on successive days testify to his failure. He receives however one gift before departure. 'Tie stones to your feet', he is told, 'pluck, though its thorns are sharp, the rose that grows on the seabed'.

And so he does. But even this hope seems lost when on the homeward journey a snake, slipping from a well, swallows the precious flower as Gilgamesh lies sleeping. That flower has a name, though: 'The old men are young again', or (most beautifully in another version) 'Rose of Heartbeat' — such a lyrical image within the bleakness of this saga. I take it as a further sign of that all-human love which Gilgamesh, heart broken at the loss of his friend, is impelled to utter. *He went a long journey… and returning engraved on a stone the whole story.* It is a grace among thorns, only to be won through binding stones to our feet.

Bedrock

Here's a stone, cold to my touch, grey and separate.
I could call it slate. That might not name it right.
It was surely embedded layer upon layer in water.

This bit of Earth has been torn from its belonging.
Now it's in my house, dry, obliged to be looked at.

I keep my self hidden. A stone though hides nothing.
Its inside is outside. It neither worries nor hurries nor
intends to hurt. I think mind imbues this grey matter.

Some nights I lie awake and pray gravity take me.
Let what I hide fall into this ground and find home.

~

*Who etched this destiny
into these bare hands?*

*One fingerprint provides
evidence that we exist.*

*Each lifeline bears a thorn
testing the truth of it.*

*Some claim the planets
appraise us as we sleep.*

*Our every hurt and joy
shares the rose's heartbeat.*

Afterword

The author and I were born on the same hour and day. Squeezed as my initials are between the names he goes by, he has invited me to appraise his poetry.

Most notably the word 'in' or its equivalents appear on almost every page. He has surely been studying some wild-eyed cabbalist who finds God's alphabet printed in the grain of wood, in hearts, in water drops, in shops and shoes and who knows what.

Precarious, too, is the maker of these poems. Since early 2017 any letters along his arteries would have met with the stent that keeps his heartbeat steady. It took a while for his ink to flow again.

You might think such a crisis would lend him gravity, but technology (though he depends on it) gets barely a mention. Oh, there may be a car or two, but so covered with cherry blossom that no one drives them. Roses pervade these pages and need pruning.

'Shake', 'giddy' and 'signature' are some further recurring words. If I question it my friend says words have a will of their own to work out their destinies.

Such personifications are infectious. Eggs talk. Walls talk. The book is full of them. He looks continually for oracles, a source beyond daytime vocabulary. Cave paintings 'speak in sleep'; the bay tree in his garden prophesies 'the end of days'. Google is my oracle. I follow the science, not poetry.

Another of my friend's obsessions is with etymology, and (reading over my shoulder) he is eager to point out that 'precarious', the word I foisted on him, once meant 'obtained by prayer', not instability.

Well, in his poem, 'Fool Proof' he tries it both ways, claiming 'high office', yet bending to admit the silliness he gives his life to. Being his guest, however, I must accommodate his giddy nonsense. Here is a crumpled verse I found under his writing desk. It won't save the planet, but at least it rhymes a bit:

> A bird on a bone
> sat thinking
> naught about nothing.
>
> Then along came Jack,
> swaggering like the Fool
> out of the old pack.
>
> Nobody knows
> how the bird spoke,
>
> but Jack in reply said:
> I inhabit each turn
> of the winding track
>
> with this stick in my hand
> and a basket full of air
> upon my back.

'A basket full of air'… is that what poetry is?

MF

About the Author

Paul Matthews has for many years been both lecturer and community poet at Emerson College in the south of England. He has travelled with his work in the USA, Australia, New Zealand, Germany, Norway, Sweden and in the UK. His explorations of the creative process come together in his creative writing sourcebook, *Sing Me the Creation*. He was the co-founder of the well-loved summer school, *Poetry OtherWise*. Gatherings of his poetry include two books from Five Seasons Press - *The Ground that Love Seeks* and *Slippery Character*s. Both are available from the author's website (see below), as is *This Naked Light* (Troubador)

www.paulmatthewspoetry.co.uk

Sing Me the Creation (Hawthorn Press)
can be ordered from Booksource:
Tel: 0141 642 9192
Email: orders@booksource.net

Further copies of *Touching Bedrock* can be ordered directly from the Troubador website or via the author's website.
Overseas readers can order from retailers such as Amazon.com

Earlier books by Paul Matthews also include:
Verge (Arc Publications)
Footnotes (Writers Forum)
Two Stones, One Bird with Owen Davis (Smith/Doorstop)
With My Heart in My Mouth (Rudolf Steiner Press)
Words in Place (Hawthorn Press)

His poem, *Waiting Outside* (p.31) was highly commended in the Bridport Poetry awards of 2022.

Acknowledgements

These poems have been published in the following journals:

Resurgence; Tears in the Fence; Scintilla; Raceme; Caduceus; New View; The Café Review.

and in these booklets, books and anthologies:

Words in Place (Hawthorn Press); *Sing Me the Creation* (Hawthorn Press); *Opening the Wolf's Skull* (Green Horse Booklet 17); *The Ground that Love Seeks* (Five Seasons Press); *PEN anthology*; *Bridport Prize anthology 2022.*

The pieces published here supersede previous versions, except for 'Love's Fabric' (p.14.) which is a less personal alternative.

'At the Boundaries' by Peter Abbs (p.65) is included by kind permission of Lisa Dart.

In 'Pondering Gilgamesh' (p.52) most of the quotations in italics are from *The Epic of Gilgamesh* (Penguin Books), translated by N.K. Sandars.

The front cover image is from the Chauvet caves in France.

Many thanks to Christine Meyer for her wood-knot photographs, and to Lee Hannam who, through her designing skills, has made all these words and images cohere.

Many friends, companions and chance acquaintances have served as touchstones for the shaping of this book, and I am grateful.

My wife Margli has been a constant and inspiring presence.

Appendix

At the Boundaries

I walk the coastal road while tavernas start to close,
the torch and scorch of summer
all but over.

Above my head the conifers rise brooding angels,
their cracked and matted wings
knotted with age.

As the sun bleeds down the sky, their blackness petrifies.
A growing and unsettling stillness.
Nothing comes back:

obscure blocks of inked stasis, innumerable turnings off,
nameless lanes plunging
down and down.

Already the white chapel on the rock has been expunged
high golden cross,
bronze bell.

At the corner house a man sits alone under an olive tree,
a low watt amber light
over his head.

I sense his shrouded body, marble shoulders, masked face.
The whole of the universe contracts
to a shudder.

I am not yet born, blind, trembling at the brink.

Peter Abbs